T0064050

IS GOD REAL?

IS GOD REAL?

IS GOD REAL?

HOW WE CAN KNOW FOR SURE

BENJAMINE V.

PARTRIDGE
A Penguin Random House Company

To order additional copies of this book, contact
Toll Free 800 101 2657 (Singapore)
Toll Free 1 800 81 7340 (Malaysia)
orders.singapore@partridgepublishing.com

www.partridgepublishing.com/singapore

Epigraph:

Question with boldness even the existence of a God; because, if there be one, he must more approve of the homage of reason, than that of blind-folded fear."

~Thomas Jefferson

CONTENTS

INTRODUCTION

Can we know if God really exists? Any honest observer will probably find fault with both the extreme monotheists *and* antitheists for the reason that they are all as confident as each other, despite the fact that one side must definitely be wrong.

I have felt the "love of God," and it is really an experience that most non-religious people do not comprehend. There is nothing like it, and it is a feeling that I can still conjure up in myself to this day. With this in mind, my de-conversion from Christianity should make absolutely no sense at all.

Truth be told, though, the *entire debate* makes no sense. Our intuitions are terrible gauges of reality. For instance, Einstein's theory of special relativity is so counter-intuitive that it may not even seem to be logically coherent. How can space and time be *different* for each individual? It would seem to make more sense that individuals might *perceive* space and time differently. Yet, without taking this fact into account, our Global Positioning System (GPS) devices would simply not work the way they do. The clocks inside the satellites are adjusted to move more quickly because time passes slower when the satellites move faster!

Nauseating libraries upon libraries of books have been produced by both sides of the God and Christianity debate, speaking one, united, ironically perplexing message: "Look! All of the evidence shows that we're right!"

I have made it my mission to navigate through the confusion, and to provide a clear road map for an honest exploration of Christian (and secular) perspectives regarding God and the Bible. By the end of this book, the confused Christian should emerge with enough certainty to continue conclusively embracing the Gospel of Jesus Christ as reality, or to conclude that it is an inaccurate claim about reality.

No matter who you are, by the end of this book, you will have enough certainty to draw confident and reliable conclusions about God, and the Christian Bible—whether you end up being for, or against them.

I challenge all readers to question every claim that is made in this book. Never accept *any* claims that do not hold up in the piercing light of an honest analysis. Just to get the ball rolling, I have provided logical guiding questions at regular intervals in Chapter 1.

Reasoning is easily clouded by good intentions.

Before I begin with the book proper, I feel it necessary to address the frame of mind that is required to grapple with the claims that I have made.

I must point out the fact that the vast majority of believers rely on the confidence of other believers to fuel *and* justify their own confidence in their beliefs, rather than relying on evidence. Of course, I do not go so far as to say that believers are unable to reason, or that they have no reason; that much is clearly untrue.

I am just pointing out that when a preacher makes a fabulously expressed claim during a sermon, the sound of a collective "amen" is enough to sway the average, well-intentioned congregation member in the direction of the provided conclusion.

After all, the preacher went to seminary, is ordained and anointed by God to preach, the sermon is a personal message from God to the member, and the congregation is full of smart people who would have noticed anything wrong with the pastor's assertions. If they—and the pastor—don't realize anything, then there probably aren't any issues to deal with, right?

When a pastor makes an extremely offensive joke about homosexuality, the whole congregation laughs along, even though some of the members realize how hurtful it may be for individuals struggling with the piercing stigma. I have, myself, been guilty of being swayed along with the crowd like this.

This is an unambiguously problematic culture that we need to deal with, but is inevitable so long as we operate within our established church structures and practices. The next time that you get an itchy feeling inside when a preacher makes a seemingly unchallengeable statement, I hope you realize that it is because there may *actually* be something wrong.

Of course, there will be a small minority of members who realize that there may be problems with whatever the preacher says. However, these observations are almost always glossed over for two main reasons: either what is said is supported by clear bible passages, or the pastor is forgiven for making a small mistake because it is relatively meaningless in the context of the "bigger picture."

Notice that, even where individuals notice problems, there is a deep-seated unwillingness to deal with bad assertions and inaccurate claims because of *good and genuine intentions* to search for deep spiritual meaning.

Therefore, the problem here is that the laudable, genuine yearning for spiritual significance clouds our better judgment, so much so that we are unable to deal transparently with the facts, and to reason our way to the conclusions that best approximate this *actual* reality that we dwell within.

The message that I'd like to communicate, then, is *not* that we should desire to destroy our hunger for spiritual significance, or to otherwise sideline our intrinsic, irremovable aching for the most ungraspable, ethereal consummations of existence that we only know how to search for in religion. Rather, we need simply to be honest with ourselves, and not let our desires cloud our judgments.

Non-religious understandings of reality that we have today almost certainly fall short of satisfying our deepest spiritual desires, but we cannot let our emotions creep past our boundaries of logic and reason, lest we become swept away by fallacies and illusions.

It is unfortunate that it is so difficult to satisfy our spiritual desires without God, but it is *worse* for us to confuse man-made fiction with testable reality. I encourage all readers to approach this book through skeptical, reasoning eyes, and do not let your biases (Yes, that includes anti-religious biases!) fool you. We can only come to better approximations of truth by testing our hypotheses against our greatest certainties about reality—not by wishing them into reality.

Why did I leave Christianity?

We require the *most* proof for those things which we value *most*. Shady characters frequently promise cures for terminal diseases, and our skepticism towards them is well justified. Notice that no amount of wishful thinking is somehow able to cause their promises to become manifest. Notice, also, that we are rightly skeptical of suspiciously promising cures, even when we know that the salesmen are well-intentioned, and otherwise very good people.

On the other hand, it is precisely *because* we are concerned with the health of our loved ones that we protect them from dangerous characters. We are not at all shameful or apologetic about interrogating their claims. Why? It is because this mechanism, which I (and many others) will call "skeptical inquiry," is our only protection from dangerous charlatans and dogma.

This, of course, does not mean that we should necessarily be confrontational or *cynical* towards every single claim that is made in our presence. Instead, we should merely be *skeptical* and tentative about truth claims, especially when they have an impact on our greatest concerns.

Some call the skeptical method of understanding the world the scientific method, and they are not wrong. The fact is that skeptical inquiry exactly means to be scientific, which is to refer to systematic and precise experimentation and observation. This leads to a misunderstanding when it is equivocated that the *academic study* of science is all that we know for sure. Clearly, that is not the case. There is still a wealth of knowledge that has yet to be truly explored by academic scientific research, especially in experiential domain, where our consciousness and spiritual experiences are concerned.

Because of the confusion between scientific *method* and the *formal* sciences (physics, biology, chemistry…), many people are oblivious to the fact that they practice the scientific method meticulously on a daily basis. It happens when we are testing medical remedies and choosing the right tutors for our students. Even children approach the world scientifically, as if by birth. Parents are the subject of their kids' experiments when the children test the limits of their parents' tolerances.

This skepticism is why I left God behind me. After nine years of being a Biblical literalist, I had to give up what I thought was real because what I learned of reality suggested otherwise. I hope that those who read this book will approach my arguments with the same kind of skepticism, and that I will be able to introduce new ways of looking at Christianity, such that the readers' perspectives will grow richer.

Of course, I realize that there are large groups of people who will arrive at completely different conclusions, based on the same observations that I have made. In fact, some people may come to the problem as skeptically as I did, and continue with even greater confidence in their faiths. There are various possible reasons for this. Yet, I still hold it to be true that, between Christianity and non-religion, one perspective is clearly superior, and we shall find out why.

Christianity makes the claim that God is a real entity; those who are non-religious make no such claims. All that remains is for us to consider the facts.

THE METHOD

In questions of science the authority of a thousand is not
worth the humble reasoning of a single individual.
~Galileo

Failure to reason

You roll a normal, six-sided die six times. What is the probability of getting all sixes? Well, the probability is one-sixth, six times, which equals one over six to the power of six. Basically, it is an impossibly small number, and we are very unlikely to observe such a result.

But does that mean that rolling six sixes is, somehow, a significant and important result? What does it mean to roll six sixes?

I propose that rolling six sixes is no different from rolling any other combination. Why? I propose this because every other possible combination is *exactly* as likely to happen; all possible combinations are exactly as likely as each other.

For instance, 6 6 6 6 6 6 is as likely as 1 2 3 4 5 6, which is as likely as 1 4 2 5 3 6, which is as likely as 2 4 1 3 6 5, and so on. The point here is that we treat statistically indistinguishable probabilities with disproportionately different degrees of importance, simply because we are human beings.

This is an example of a systemic flaw in human reasoning. We are imprisoned, by our nature, to minds with flaws that cannot be resolved. We are only able to *circumvent* these flaws in human reasoning by identifying them, and then acknowledging that those methods of "reasoning" do not square with reality. For example, pilots sometimes encounter "false horizons" in the sky, but are trained to ignore them, and to pay attention to what the plane's instruments communicate to the pilot instead.

If you have seen demonstrations of optical illusions, then you will be familiar with how we are easily fooled by our eyes. Even when we are aware of the fact that there is an illusion at work, we cannot help but feel as if the illusion is real.

Just as pilots learn to use aeronautic instruments to navigate the skies, we, too, must learn to navigate the debate over God and reality with an illusion-proofed tool. This requires us to refine our method of reasoning. Let's begin with an analogy.

An analogy

Suppose that God is real and can provide supernatural healing, but that prayer does not work. God is not significantly handicapped by this because he might have other methods of allowing somebody to seek supernatural healing. Nevertheless, attempting to pray can yield no other result than a placebo effect.

For those who are unfamiliar, the placebo effect refers to the phenomenon that occurs when somebody's *belief* in a cause is responsible for a result. Patients who participate in double-blinded drug trials are randomly given "placebos," sometimes referred to as "sugar pills," instead of the drug under consideration, to ensure that any improvements are caused by the drug, as opposed to their *belief* in that drug. In this analogy, I have proposed that praying will not yield any results except those that are caused by a *belief* in the effect of prayer.

In this hypothetical situation, I am, sadly, diagnosed with a very horrible strand of polio. On top of that, I may only decide to pursue one method of treatment. I may either have a (modern) mainstream medical treatment, or pray for healing. Due to my misinterpretation of the Bible, I believe that prayer is superior to "scientific" methods. I choose to pray, and die a very unfortunate death. We can continue to assume that, had I chosen the other, I would have likely been swiftly cured by the medicine.

Again, I must clarify that this is a purely hypothetical situation, and we are *assuming* that God cannot heal through prayer for the purposes of this example.

There are many lenses through which we try to understand human misjudgment. Here, I think that the context of problem-solving is a very useful perspective to take. Through this lens, we understand that all decisions made by people are done to solve problems.

What methods to we have to solve problems? I am not sure that there is more than one proper solution. Clearly, we are limited to the faculties of our senses and reason. The only way that we know how to solve problems is through the experience of sight, sound, smell, touch, and taste, filtered and explained through our minds.

In my hypothetical situation, I am misled by failing to properly reason. I could have also arrived at the same outcome if my senses were hijacked. For instance, friends might tell me stories about people who were cured of diseases after they prayed, leaving out the important detail that these cured people represent an unfairly small proportion of those who decided to pray, and that the rest subsequently passed away.

We are forced to accept that even the best sensory input and reasoning will not always provide us with sufficient or correct information. However, if we do not rely on these, *then what can we trust?*

Let's say that I could clearly listen to the Abrahamic God, who could speak audibly into my conscious mind. Even if that were true, I would still be relying on that voice on the basis of reason, which would still, in turn, be justified by consistently positive results, observed through my five senses. My conclusion, then, is that we are *only able to rely* on our senses and reasoning.

This is very important to acknowledge. We are easily misled by our senses, and easily swayed by false reasoning. It is not surprising that any of us should be wrong about a million things at any given time. Yet, reasoning is all that we have. We are slaves to reason, but there is nothing else to obey; reason is the *only* way to go about understanding the world.

Checkpoint
Question Everything

1. Was this really a sensible, useful, or applicable analogy? How might it be wrong or misleading?
2. Are we "clearly" limited to our faculties of senses and reason? What other faculties are at our disposal, and how consistently effective are they in comparison to our senses and reason?

Evidence is confusing.

Both sides of this debate should be greatly humbled by the reminder that even the most irrational of the conspiracy theorists (which is saying something) can find "evidence" for aliens who have made their way to Earth, sometimes forming the Illuminati, and are disguised amongst us as American illegal immigrants (and politicians!)—and their evidence *does* sound convincing when they're speaking. Of course, most of us have not concluded similarly, despite the fact that they can produce *convincing* "evidence."

"Following the evidence" will not get us anywhere useful until a method is put in place to keep our reasoning processes in check. We are all too easily fooled. Here are three reasons why:

1: Everybody can produce evidence for their side.

Do you have evidence "against God?" I can find you evidence "for God." If our concern is merely to "find evidence," then we will all be greatly confused by the information. This is especially the case because both sides of the debate have been producing evidence for the past 2000 years.

2: Not all evidence is relevant or useful.

Lawyers say that this kind of evidence is "immaterial" evidence (not relevant to the case). For example, say that I am put on trial for robbing a bank. The prosecution asserts that I am the guilty, and decides to prove it by showing that I watch a lot of bank robbery movies. This would prove that I enjoy watching dramatized bank robberies, but does nothing to prove that I robbed that bank. Of course, it might still be useful to throw this evidence out there, if for no other purpose except for swaying the emotions of the jury. Nevertheless, it does not change the fact that I did not rob the bank.

3: Asserted conclusions do not always follow from the evidence provided.

Some monotheists claim that God's existence is evidenced by how bananas are "designed" to "perfectly" fit in our hands. On the other hand, some atheists claim that God's inexistence is evidenced by how their own prayers are left unanswered. Both examples illustrate conclusions that have been unnecessarily extrapolated from otherwise unrelated "evidences."

Checkpoint
Question Everything

1. Is evidence really this confusing, or are these observations misleading?
2. If true at all, to what extent are these claims true?

How to find clarity in confusion

There is a way to avoid these pitfalls of human reasoning. In order to understand reality better, we are required to define a method to test our interpretations of reality. This way, we can be certain that we approach reality from the perspective that is the best.

How can we do this?

Firstly, our foundations must rely on the same assumption: only one position is viable. That is to say that God (monotheism) cannot exist *and* not exist (atheism) at the same time—neither can God be 'everything and everywhere,' (pantheism) while simultaneously being non-existent. As a result, only one position's arguments should stand the test of rigorous evaluation, in the light of all other possible options.

Secondly, rigorous evaluations require rigorous criteria. Our positions (hypotheses):

1. must be clearly defined (under X conditions, Y actions will have a Z result),
2. must be *repeatedly* testable,
3. and must be *consistently* better at predicting results than other positions.

Thirdly, hypotheses should be tested through this process:

1. Form a hypothesis (as above).
2. Test the hypothesis with an experiment (create X conditions, expecting Z or other result).
3. Ensure that the results (Z or otherwise) of this experiment are reproducible. If not, refine the hypothesis *or* process and repeat step 2.
4. Show that the hypothesis has either been proved or disproved (under X conditions, Y actions will have a Z result).
5. This entire process must be repeatable so that others can draw the same conclusions.

Here is an example of a good hypothesis, and how its analysis would produce a useful conclusion for us:

- I have a coin. One side is heads, and the other is tails.
- Step 1: I hypothesize that, all other factors remaining equal, when I flip the coin into the air, it will land on my hand heads side up.
- Step 2: I flip the coin. It lands tails side up.
- Step 3: I flip the coin again 5 times. It sometimes lands heads side up, and sometimes tails side up.
- Step 3: Since the results are inconsistent, I may either refine the hypothesis or experiment. Let's say that I refine both. I now hypothesize that, all other factors remaining equal, when I flip the coin into the air, it *must always* land on my hand heads side up. My experiment changes in that I flip the coin 10 times.

- Repeat step 2: I flip the coin 10 times, and it lands heads side up 5 times.
- Step 4: The coin landed tails side up 5 out of 10 times. Therefore, the hypothesis that the coin "must always land on my hand heads side up" is not true. It is, then, *disproved*.
- Step 5: Suppose that I *happened to* get a result where the coin landed heads side up every time. I would have inaccurately proved the hypothesis. That is why entire process is supposed to be repeatable. That way, if I got a bit skeptical of the result, I could do it again, and realize that my previous results were merely caused by a lucky streak. On top of that, all of my friends would be able to prove me wrong.

You may recognize this approach as the "scientific method." As I've already said in the introduction, it is sometimes claimed that this method is one of many similarly reliable approaches that are available. It makes the situation worse that the word "science" is in the term "scientific method," since the connotations get all mixed up.

Is it really true, then, that the scientific method (or skeptical inquiry) is one of many similarly reliable methods to discover truths about reality? If there are, I have not found any of them.

If you are considering a possibility, test that process against anything that you know conclusively to be true, and then see if it is as consistently reliable as the scientific method. For example, see if you use that process to test the hypothesis that gravity is real, or that water boils at 100 degrees Celsius.

Every usable example of modern technology is a fruit of the scientific method, including the computer that I am typing this book on. Here are two examples of fruits of the scientific method, which could not have otherwise been designed using "other methods."

Your LCD screen

In the 1800s, Thomas Young and Hermann von Helmholtz used the scientific method to show us that our eyes see the spectrum of light (often abbreviated as ROYGBIV) as a mix of red, green, and blue.

That means that human eyes have trouble distinguishing between a light source that is genuinely orange, and a light source that is orange because of a mix of red and green lights. We can, therefore, fool our eyes into seeing the entire spectrum of colors of light by mixing red, green, and blue lights.

My screen is an LCD screen, which produces images by lighting up a grid of individual colors, called pixels. To be exact, my own screen is composed of a grid of 1366 by 768 pixels, where each pixel is producing the exact color that is dictated by the computer.

How does each pixel produce the exact color specified if the light source in the screen is white? Well, each pixel has three colored filters with electronically adjustable levels, and the filters are respectively colored—you guessed it—red, green, and blue!

On its own, the hypothesis made by Young and Helmholtz would have probably seemed a little odd to most people. Yet, because of the scientific method, civilizations were able to collectively agree that it was true. Two centuries later, we owe the production of our mobile gadgets to people like Young and Helmholtz, who made crazy guesses about reality, and tested them with the scientific method.

The atomic bomb

Here's one example that really drives the point home. Try building one of these things through a "non-naturalistic approach."

In 1905, Albert Einstein published a scientific paper containing a seemingly insane idea. He hypothesized that mass could be converted to energy, and that energy could be converted to mass, without losing any parts of that physical system. In other words, he proposed mass-energy equivalence. Most of us recognize this concept in formula form as $E=MC^2$.

He was not the first scientist to make this sort of guess. However, he was the first to craft a formula (that was accurate!) to define the exact proportion by which mass and energy are related (the speed of light, squared). This formula can be derived on paper, provided that we assume some preexisting knowledge about physics, but that's not the starkest form of proof that we can provide.

40 years later, the United States of America used this otherwise seemingly trivial knowledge to construct and drop atomic bombs on Hiroshima and Nagasaki. In total, at least 150,000 people were killed, equivalent to the number of people who have died between 2011 and 2014 in the Syrian Civil War (which is ongoing as I write this book).

It did not matter that mass-energy equivalence was difficult for most people to understand. It did not even matter that it was confusing and counter-intuitive. Einstein's ideas were rigorously tested with the scientific method, and they were found to be accurate on the basis of stringent analyses and experimentation.

It is interesting to note that this *approach* is actually counter-intuitive for some people, in comparison to 'honestly exploring the evidence.' It turns out that we can have vastly different interpretations of 'honestly exploring.'

I propose that we *can* conclude with reliable and actionable certainty that God either exists or does not exist, just as we could test the Young-Helmholtz theory of trichromatic color vision and Einstein's theory of mass-energy equivalence. We can do so by rigorously evaluating the multiple hypotheses that are possible.

Checkpoint
Question Everything

1. Must only one position or claim be viable at any moment?
2. Is it *actually* effective to put a system of "rigorous" testing in place? Are there better ways to test what we think we know?
3. How far is it *possible* or *useful* for us to apply the scientific method to test the existence of God, or the truth of Biblical claims?

What about metaphysical claims?

I have demonstrated that the scientific method is effective in testing the validity of scientific claims. Translation: the scientific method is a good method for doing science. In other words, it may seem like I have not said anything particularly useful at all. There are two areas of interest that we have not yet explored.

Here is the first question, which is one that many people ask: how can we possibly use a method for understanding the *physical* world to understand a *metaphysical* God? Indeed, if we assume that God is purely metaphysical, then physical methods of testing are probably not going to work very well.

This is one of the more succinct and eloquent defenses regarding the testability of Biblical claims. However, this defense suffers a flaw in logic, in that it distorts the original proposal that has been made.

I have not yet heard anybody proposing that it is either possible *or* useful to apply the scientific method to directly test the claim of a metaphysical God. Rather, it is proposed that (and *has always been* proposed that) we should use the scientific method to test the *physical* claims that are made by Christianity, regarding acts of creation, critical historical events, and so on.

A conjuring trick—intentional or not—has been performed right under our noses, switching the original proposal for a fake one. The fancy, technical, philosophical term for the fake proposal is "straw man." It means that the original argument is distorted before it is attacked, so that it will look like the argument has been defeated.

We have, then, established that claims are, indeed, testable with the scientific method, so long as they are *physical* claims. Now, on to the second question: what about *real* metaphysical claims?

It is now immediately clear that we have moved into the territory of many voices, and much confusion (as if things have not been confusing enough). In order to deal with this question cleanly, let's think about what "metaphysical" actually means.

What does metaphysical mean to you? What examples can you come up with? That seems to be the best way to go about this. Take a minute to think up examples.

This is where I encounter an obstacle that I am not able to cross. I simply cannot come up with any *truly* metaphysical claims that make any sense. The closest that I am able to get to "metaphysical" is "God is love." Yet, even in this case, a physical claim has been implicitly made. Let's take a look at what "God is love" means:

1. God is love.
2. God, only being love, must always perform acts of love; otherwise, God is not, and cannot be, love.
3. We can say that any act that is attributable to God must be one of love.

The implication of a claim like this being made is that we are *able* to disprove it. If we identify something as an act of God, and it is demonstrably evil, then we can conclude that "God is [not] love." As a result, I come to the following conclusion regarding metaphysical claims: if a claim is useful to me in any way, it *must be* a physical claim. Another way of phrasing it is this: a truly metaphysical claim is not a useful or meaningful claim to me.

Checkpoint
Question Everything

1. Is my method of defining "metaphysical" sufficient? Are there better ways to demarcate the boundaries between physical and metaphysical?
2. Provided that we conclusively identify an act of God, and demonstrate that it is evil, is the claim "God is love" actually disproved, as I have suggested?
3. What is an example of a useful metaphysical claim? Is that a logical possibility?

Taking the first step

There are two pivotal chapters in this book: the first (this one), and Unconscionable Morality. Anybody can claim to be objective, and to "seek evidence." Yet, methods of seeking evidence vary by individuals and philosophies. How will we decide to approach the question of God?

In this chapter, I have laid out a proposed method of viewing the facts. Let me reiterate and summarize it as best as I can:

1. Begin with a claim; for example, "hydrated runners are better at running."
2. Clarify, or simplify the claim, so that it is understandable by as many observers as possible; for example, "sufficiently-hydrated sprinters sprint faster than dehydrated sprinters."

3. Define what you expect will happen when your hypothesis is true, and what you expect will happen when your hypothesis is false. This is very important, so make sure that the criteria makes sense. In this case, I would not agree that every individual will necessarily sprint faster when sufficiently-hydrated than when dehydrated. Instead, I would say that, on average, sprinters who are sufficiently-hydrated will sprint faster than when they are dehydrated, assuming that all other factors remain constant.

4. Design a test that will either prove or disprove the hypothesis.

5. Perform the test, and get others to repeat it.

6. Consistent results imply that a conclusion can be made.

I have shown that this is the best way to approach any claims that have been made about this universe. It forces us to lay aside our biases and disagreements, and it forces us to commit to results. The real trouble is when we begin to deviate from our principles. With both rational and irrational people on both sides of this debate, we cannot risk deviation from rational inquiry.

How committed will you be to the evidence? Will you change your mind if it shows that you are wrong? What if God really *does* exist? What if he really doesn't? Let's find out what the evidence has shown us.

DEAR BELIEVER

I f the reader skips every single chapter in this book but one, then this is the chapter that should be read. Here, I have condensed my best, and most relevant points into a single letter, written to my Christian friends. The debate can always go on, and there is always something else to say, but I have made it my mission, over the past two years, to condense an entire argument against Christianity into one chapter. I call it my "concise argument against Christianity."

Dear Believer,

There are both rational and irrational people on both sides of the debate regarding the Christian God and Bible. It has been hotly debated for the past 2000 years, and there still seems to be no consensus. Christians and non-Christians, alike, are able to go about living from the consequences of their conclusions about God and the Bible, as if their conclusions are based on a sufficient analysis of the facts concerning Christianity.

Assuming that we have all *looked at the facts*, then either:

1. Neither of the sides are able to make consistent, rational conclusions based on the facts,
2. Or one side is wrong about their analysis of the facts available.

The first possibility means that the data is inconclusive. If that is true, then we can neither conclude that God is real, nor conclude that the Bible is the divinely-inspired Word of God. This is because the extraordinary burden of proof is on the one making the extraordinary claim.

Bertrand Russell's celestial teapot argument helps us to wrap our minds around this idea. He would claim that there was a china teapot revolving around the sun, in an orbit between the Earth and Mars. If he asserted this to us, it would not be our prerogative to *disprove* it with evidence. The burden of proof, therefore, is on the one making the claim. If he could not prove it, then we would be led to conclude that there is no such thing.

If the first possibility were the case, then the debate would end there. Therefore, I have written the following points assuming the second possibility.

From a non-religious perspective

I acknowledge that a Christian and non-Christian will not approach this problem with the same frame of mind. The Christian operates with extremely deeply seated and sensitive assumptions about God, and these assumptions have far reaching effects, which are pivotal to the way that the Christian leads his life. In some cases, nearly all life-changing decisions pivot around these assumptions.

As a result, I realize that I cannot only provide one perspective. This first one will be of an impartial observer, while the second "perspective" will be a more aggressive and thorough argument. That is because I have acknowledged that a Christian will require more motivation to relinquish these assumptions, which he already holds dear to himself.

In order to understand the answers that we are looking for, we are required to ask the right questions. In this case, I will pose two questions:

1. Is the Bible divinely-inspired?
2. Is the gospel of Jesus Christ sufficiently substantiated by historical evidence?

In both cases, I am able to pose specific hypotheses. Each hypothesis will encompass specific criteria that allow the hypotheses to be falsified. We can then look at the evidence, and then conclude that the hypotheses are either confirmed, or disproved. Let's deal with them one at a time.

1. Is the Bible divinely-inspired?

What kind of hypotheses can we form for such a significant claim? Many hypotheses have been presented by various philosophers and theologians, but most of these arguments have not been conclusive because debaters are constantly disagreeing on the *criteria* for suitable evidence.

For instance, it has been proposed that we can conclude that the Bible is not divinely-inspired if and when we can produce evidence of just one contradiction in the Bible. Christians continue to claim that all produced contradictions are only purported contradictions, and are actually not, while non-Christians continue to argue that they are. The debate never ends.

I will propose a hypothesis that is easier to understand and test, based on one that is still being hotly debated. This is my hypothesis:

If the Bible is divinely-inspired, then it should contain at least one example of a testable revelation that its writers could not have otherwise known or guessed.

For example, if the Bible told us (before anybody did mathematics) that the areas and circumferences of circles were related to the lengths and squares their radii and diameters by a number that could be rounded off to 3.14159, then we would have cause to believe that there was some kind of divine (or, at least, greater than human) inspiration behind the Bible.

We could also conclude similarly if the Bible told us that all types of Earthly life (all known living things) are constructed on the basis of a molecular language with four letters, forming a double-helix structure.

The prophecy of a divinely-ordained, sovereign state, for example, does not count because it would not be a difficult "revelation" to imagine. The above two examples conform to the criteria that the authors of the Biblical cannon "could not have otherwise known or guessed" them.

I will leave the conclusions of this test to the reader to decide.

2. *Is the gospel of Jesus Christ sufficiently substantiated by historical evidence?*

Again, debates have not ended regarding this question, chiefly because the two sides tend to disagree on the criteria necessary to demonstrate that the given hypotheses are valid. I will attempt to provide a concise, understandable, and clear hypothesis.

If the gospel of Jesus Christ is substantiated by historical evidence, then (1) Jesus' resurrection should be scientifically provable, and (2) the most dramatic events in the gospels should have significant extra-Biblical corroboration.

These are not unrealistically high expectations. If we are not able to prove a resurrection (1), then we have no reason to conclude that it happened, since anecdotal evidence does not suffice in substantiating such an extraordinary claim (a physical and scientific claim, no less). However, it may be helpful, if for no other reason than to do so, to acknowledge that the existing evidence:

1. Suggests that there was probably a figure who we might or might not be able to name "Jesus Christ of Nazareth,"
2. And that such a figure had a sizable religious following.

Even if the first criteria ("Jesus' resurrection should be scientifically provable") is not met, the second criteria still leaves us wanting. Although I assume that most Christians will probably turn to apologists who claim to have significant extra-Biblical evidence for Jesus' ministry, I refer to events such as the *mass resurrection* in Matthew 27:52-53, which are simply not accounted for.

So what?

I have posed two questions, and provided specific hypotheses as tests for both of them. I would like to reiterate that, in the case that data does not conclusively support the conclusions that are asserted, then the conclusions cannot be logically made, even if the data points in that direction, since we are still forced by the data to arrive at a different conclusion (that the claims of Christianity remain unsubstantiated, and therefore untrue).

I have found that the evidence does not sufficiently support the claims of (1) a divinely-inspired Bible, and (2) the gospel of Jesus Christ, as reported by the writers of the four gospels. Furthermore, the provided evidence may, in fact, suggest a tellingly anthropocentric Bible, and the existence of an otherwise normal religious movement.

Therefore, as someone with no vested interest in returning to or having anything significantly to do with Christianity, I find no reason to dig further into the claims that have been made. However, I understand that further investigation may be necessary for a Christian to change his positions on such central beliefs. That is what we will be dealing with next.

From a Christian perspective

These arguments are meant to challenge the Christian perspective, so as to reveal that the Christian position is not based on solid reasoning or proof. Christians should (rightfully) read this with a healthy degree of skepticism, in the same fashion that all claims should be approached.

1. Burden of proof

I reiterate that the burden of proof to demonstrate the validity of Christian claims is on the Christian himself, and not on the opposite party, although I will still do so in the following points for the sake of being thorough.

The Christian is left to substantiate a breadth of extraordinary claims. Here are four examples:

1. God exists.
2. The Universe was created by God.
3. Jesus resurrected.
4. Miracles happen(ed), depending on your denomination.

It is unsettling and suspicious that many of these claims are, at once, both conveniently unprovable and unfalsifiable, based on standards set by Christian apologists.

2. Biblical argument about morality of God

The burden of proof is on the Christian, but it is also possible to disprove the morality of the Christian God. This is possible because there are fundamentally unchallengeable assumptions that Christians must make. The one that is most relevant to this point is that:

The God of Christianity (the God of the Bible) is perfectly just.

The result of this claim is that, if we can provide an example of God not being perfectly just in the Bible, then that God cannot exist. We are unable to rule out other types of gods or types of "God," but the God that is of concern to us cannot possibly exist.

There are many examples of Biblical passages that can be listed, but only one is necessary, so I will cite the example that is most vivid to me.

Read Numbers 31. It will be best to do so before reading my summary, since I don't intend to add any details that are untrue. In it, God (through Moses, but clearly God nonetheless) commands the Israelites to kill all of the Midianites because some of the Israelites and Midianites fornicated with each other. The Israelites return from battle with all the spoils of Midian, and with the remaining women and children of Midian in captivity.

When the Israelites return with the women and children of Midian, God says through Moses: "Have you allowed all the women to live?" (NIV). The Israelites are then commanded to finish off the women and children, although they are also conveniently told to keep the virgin girls for themselves.

Just to make the message really clear, imagine what it would be like for one of us to walk into a neighbor's house with a machete, stab the man of the household to death, steal the family's belongings, kidnap the woman, daughter, and infant boy, stab the woman and baby boy to death at home, and then force the sixteen year old daughter into a God-ordained message, for the reason that you had an affair with the woman of that house.

Details aside, the salient point here is that God has clearly commanded genocide several times in the Bible, and His commands have been willingly, consistently, and successfully executed, with no rebuke from God. Notice that the "purify[ing]" commands which follow the commands of genocide do nothing to justify the genocide.

The analogy may be a useful guide to understanding this. Planning to shower off the blood stains that *I plan to cause* neither purifies me, nor justifies the actions that I consciously intend to commit.

I have read several arguments that attempt to justify God's commands in Numbers 31 to kill the Midianites. None of them justify these actions. The best of the arguments may, however, cause the actions to possibly be admissible. However, the key distinction that must be made here is between actions that are *justifiable*, and *admissible*.

It may be admissible to brutally torture a terrorist to a gut-wrenching death, or to perform female genital mutilation on an innocent, virgin girl, if we can somehow guarantee the prevention of a million, otherwise unnecessary deaths (whether caused by Earthly bombs, or by supernatural plagues). However, we would *never* feel that such an action could be *justified*.

My conclusion regarding Numbers 31 is that God's commands here (and elsewhere) to cause genocide are inexcusable. Even if we only attributed the genocide of the Midianite men to God (as opposed to the entire mission of pillaging), it would still be *unjustifiable, inexcusable, and unconscionable*.

Since the diction of the scriptures clearly identifies God as the source of the command of genocide (here and elsewhere), we can conclude that the God of the Bible is not "perfectly just." Therefore, God is either (1) non-existent, or (2) not the perfectly just God that we think we know. Neither conclusions allow us to continue being Christians.

3. Moral argument from salvation

Interestingly, I suspect that this line of reasoning could be applied effectively to test the reasonability of other supernatural claims. It is essentially a drawn-out analysis of the Christian method of salvation (in the narrow context that salvation means to escape damnation and enter heaven) that suggests that the character understood to be the Christian god could not have created this gospel. My condensed argument is this:

A sufficiently loving and just god would not leave us without a suitable tool to decisively show (or at least suggest) which religion leads legitimately to eternal life (or away from damnation). It can also be said that, assuming one of the religions is true, God has left us unable to decisively escape eternal damnation.

Above, I deliberately took some context away so that I could distill my argument down to its shortest version. Here is a longer, more carefully explained version of the same thing, which should more comprehensively get the message across:

P1. A loving and just God will provide a fair, identifiable path to salvation for the honest seeker.

P2. Salvation is attained by different and incompatible methods amongst the 3 Abrahamic faiths.

P3. The consequence of not attaining salvation is of eternal significance, if true.

P4. The 3 faiths cannot be simultaneously correct. Only 1 can be true.

P5. The 3 faiths are neither conclusively provable nor disprovable, either individually or against each other, within some reasonable doubt.

C1. Therefore, there is no reasonable way for one to deduce which specific path is certainly the correct path to salvation (from premises 2 and 5).

C2. Therefore, if one of the faiths were true, God would have effectively failed to provide a fair path to salvation for the honest seeker (from conclusion 1). The misled believer, having honestly chosen wrongly, would be punished in the hell of whichever respective religion were actually true (from premises 2, 3, and 4).

C3. Therefore, there is no such type of God responsible for the creation of any of these 3 faiths (from premise 1 and conclusion 2).

Notice that God does not merely fail to provide a fair path to salvation for the honest seeker. In doing so, he paves a path which unfairly and horrifically ends in an eternity of suffering and torture for every single person who has been, is, or will be unluckily and helplessly categorized as "unsaved," while some of the worst sinners in history will, through no merit of their own, enjoy an eternity of bliss and satisfaction.

4. Pascal's Wager

Argument 1 demonstrates that the Christian does not have any sufficiently demonstrable basis to make his claims. Arguments 2 and 3 disprove crucial Christian assumptions. Based on all of the available data, we see that it is unreasonable to hold a Christian position.

However, it is not uncommon for Christians to continue holding their positions, for fear that God may still be real. There are two ways that this is articulated:

1. Maybe the data is inconclusive, and more data will come in later to show that I am right. (My response: see argument one. That only leaves us with the second option as a possibility.)
2. Should I not still believe, just in case hell really exists?

The second option is Pascal's Wager. Here is my response to Pascal's Wager:

We recognize that we do not make decisions like this based purely on the reliability of reason and evidence. Another major factor that molds our decisions is potential outcome. Clearly, nobody gambles on the lottery on the rational basis that they will likely win, since that result is unambiguously not the case. Instead, we are willing to gamble because of the potential consequences.

I struggled with this idea, as many people do, but did not arrive at the same conclusion as Blaise Pascal. Pascal's Wager argues that we should wager to believe in God on the basis that the potential gain heavily outweighs the potential loss of not believing in God, which is to say, heaven and hell. It seems to be a reasonable gamble, but, as many philosophers have pointed out, it suffers from miscalculations on more than one level. I will explain three mistakes that I have, myself, found the argument to make:

Firstly, we approach gambling and philosophy with different objectives in mind. Gambling games are played to maximize outcome, so it is both necessary and useful to take probability and the probable outcomes into account (a 10% chance of winning $100 is effectively the same option as a 100% chance of winning $10). On the other hand, so long as choices of belief are made with the purpose of reflecting reality, it is neither necessary nor useful to take the values of the potential outcomes into account ($100 vs $10). The mistake, therefore, is that the assumption is made that we choose beliefs to maximize outcome, rather than to reflect reality as closely as possible (10% vs 100%).

Secondly, this method of reasoning is questionable insofar as it disregards the importance of probability, even if we hold the assumption that choices of belief are made to maximize outcome. This is because maximizing the outcome of a wager requires the subject to compare choices by multiplying their respective outcomes and probabilities.

One way to illustrate this second fallacy is to propose a perfect outcome with an absolute zero probability of resulting. As a result of the calculation, the perfect outcome becomes useless because anything multiplied by zero is still zero. This means that any value will yield the exact same result, when combined with this probability. In such a situation, there is no good reason to make this wager over any other possible wager, except when all other outcomes have a net-negative result, which is to say that it is only useful to choose a zero that is certain when all else is also certainly zero or negative.

Thirdly, Pascal's Wager fails to adhere to its own logic because it does not account for the fact that there are other positions with potential outcomes that are unquestionably superior. The argument proposes that we should decide on the Christian position, which has neither the most enticing rewards, nor the most fearful punishments.

Even when well-established examples of such positions become under dispute, we may still show that this wager is flawed by introducing a self-imagined system of supernatural beliefs that fulfils these criteria (better rewards and fiercer punishments). The result would be that, since probability is not taken into account, Pascal's logic causes us to decide that it is reasonable to believe in that self-imagined system, which is clearly an undesirable result. We can, therefore, conclude that, of the logic and application of Pascal's Wager, at least one of these two things is flawed, if not both.

5. Christianity is not contributing

I have invalidated the argument that it is reasonable to take Christianity as a tentative position, in the absence of better evidence to prove it. I will now propose that Christianity is, in fact, not useful to us. I will do this by examining the usefulness of Christian ideas.

First, let's define the boundaries between what is identifiably Christian, and what is not identifiably Christian. To define anything is to specify exactly what that "thing" is, to a point where this description cannot apply to anything else. Something identifiably Christian cannot also be identifiably Jewish, Islamic, Hindu, Spiritualist, or secular.

For instance, the doctrine of grace, or "unmerited favor," is not identifiably Christian unless we insert the name of Jesus. Replacing the name of Jesus with any other name allows us to make that idea a non-Christian idea. There is no specific detail about this doctrine that leads us to believe that it can be claimed as the exclusive dominion of Christianity, except when we are speaking only of religion. In that case, we might make the case that it is an identifiably Christian religious idea. Of course, even this is a difficult case to make.

This example allows us to conclude that an "identifiably Christian idea" is one which only Christianity can claim ownership of. However, it is not yet clear as to what constitutes a positive example of an idea that can be identifiably claimed for ownership by any single entity.

Here is an example of an identifiably mathematical idea. Modern algebra was developed by Muslim scholars during the Golden Age of Islam. However, algebra is not identifiably Muslim because it is a central methodology that is shared by all mathematicians. We can, therefore, call it an identifiably mathematical idea, because it requires us to make assumptions that are mathematical by definition (for example: all valid equations can be mathematically manipulated without destroying any mathematical symmetries).

As previously stated, the objective of this argument is to show that Christianity is not useful to us. In order to do so, I will first show how other ideas (not identifiably Christian) have been useful to us.

The scientific method has been responsible for every major medical advance in the history of modern medicine, by testing, and then confirming or disproving hypotheses that were uncontestably physiochemical. The scientific method worked across religious and spiritual boundaries, and many of the discoverers of medical breakthroughs were, themselves, Christian, such as Louis Pasteur, whose pivotal contributions to science included contributions to germ theory, vaccination, and pasteurization. A few of these major breakthroughs include the germ theory, antiviral drugs, vaccinations, cancer treatments, and the eradication of smallpox (and polio is not far away).

When sectarian (or "alternative") ideas become demonstrably useful, they cease to be alternative. That has always been the case, regardless of the fields to which the contributions go to. We have examined examples relevant to mathematics, physics, chemistry, biology, economics, and medicine.

Are there any situations in which identifiably Christian ideas have something significant to contribute? I only know of two claims, and neither of them are convincing to me.

Firstly, it is often claimed that Christianity is responsible for very great proportions of charitable contributions to society.

My response to this claim is that I cannot distinguish between this "Christianity" and altruism. If I take away the altruism in the equation, have I taken away a person's Christianity? And if altruism is the result of Christianity, then there must surely be some situation where a person's Christianity has not yet moved them to be so measurably charitable. In other words, I have not seen any identifiably Christian ideas.

Secondly, it is also claimed that Christianity is responsible for the moral uprightness of modern society.

Again, I am unable to distinguish between Christianity here, and moral uprightness here, if we choose to hypothesize that Christianity is responsible for moral uprightness. Can we not have moral uprightness without referencing Jesus' death and resurrection? I'm not sure that any identifiably Christian ideas are relevant in a discussion regarding capital punishment.

Furthermore, to claim that Christianity is exclusively responsible for the moral uprightness of modern society is to forget about the enlightenment, the rise of secular political and moral philosophy, the advancements of science, and the emergence of the educated middle class. If we acknowledge the relevance of forces like these, then how can we be so certain that our morality is the exclusive result of Christianity?

This entire argument about the irrelevance of Christianity is really here to challenge a deep-seated, implicit assumption about Christianity: that Christianity is good for us.

As it is with the rest of the assumptions that I have challenged here, this is a claim that nobody is obliged to assume is true. The (extraordinary) burden of proof is on the Christian, and I have yet to see any convincing proof.

6. Line in the sand

Argument 1 demonstrates that the Christian does not have any sufficiently demonstrable basis to make his claims. Arguments 2 and 3 disprove crucial Christian assumptions. Argument 4 invalidates the argument that Christianity should be taken as a tentative position. Argument 5 makes it uncomfortably evident that Christianity is irrelevant. Based on all of the available data, we see that it is unreasonable to hold a Christian position.

Point 6 is not so much of an argument, as it is a call to action. I pose a simple question to the Christian:

What, and how much, information do you require to decide that you are wrong? Can you know if you are wrong?

Where do you draw the line, and has it been crossed?

Unconscionable Morality

Moral questions are particularly significant because they hit at the heart of one of the (if not the) most important functions of religion: moral guidance. If we assume that Christianity is true, then we should expect it to follow that the Christian Bible preaches a perfect morality, and that this morality does not come into conflict with the moral compass that God would have built into us.

The primary defense that Christians bring up against the incompatibilities that I have pointed out is that the Bible is more description than prescription, which is to say that it does more to *describe* the morality of its characters than to *prescribe* a certain kind of morality to its readers.

I have mentioned this because I feel that it is disingenuous to categorize verses and passages as descriptive rather than prescriptive simply because the extracts come into conflict with the readers' moral intuitions. This is especially the case when these kinds of arguments come in the form of "context" arguments, proposing that their meanings are read out of context, when, clearly, they are *not*.

One example of this kind of conflict is what arises when Abraham's sacrifice of Isaac at Moriah is mentioned. God unambiguously commands Abraham to "offer [Isaac] there for a burnt offering..."[1] Regardless of what your moral intuitions and interpretations are, it should be very obvious that God is not at all disgusted by this kind of action.

Some will rise to the defense of God's command by claiming that the verse is read out of context, and that it should be understood through typology (as in a foreshadowing allegory of the New Testament). The problem is that this kind of argument, even if true, fails to exempt God from the responsibility of commanding Abraham to burn his own son.

No arguments, including the typological and metaphorical, exempt any Godly commands of morality from responsibility. Therefore, we should read the Bible's moral commands as purely prescriptive, and understand that any other meanings, even if true, are additional.

Confident claims about morality in the Bible often contradict an innate sense of morality.

It is a common understanding that the Bible teaches morals, and that it provides wisdom, whether truly 'revealed'

---

[1]   Genesis 22:2 (KJV)

or not. After all, many good people have claimed to draw moral and practical wisdom from the Christian Bible. I think that we take this expectation for granted, assuming that the entire Bible sets a high bar for moral conduct.

Of course, this expectation is well-justified. Preachers teach us that Jesus, being God, was so good that he rebuked Pharisees for their hypocrisy,[2] and imparted moral wisdom to edify those humble enough to listen.[3] We read that God, through Old Testament law, enforced such great holiness that people contaminated by unholy sin would be quarantined away from the rest of the Israelites, lest their sin further contaminate the camp.[4]

On the other hand, there is clearly a lot of violence and suffering in the Bible, and it is problematic.

Much of it can be (and has rightfully been) attributed to human fallibility. David autonomously commits adultery with Bathsheba,[5] and Judas willingly betrays Jesus.[6]

Yet, we are faced with some stories that leave us scratching our heads in confusion. Abraham provides a human sacrifice—his son, no less—at the command of God.[7] Time after time, the Israelites, under the command of God, commit blatant genocide for disproportionately insignificant reasons.

---

[2]   Matthew 23:13

[3]   Matthew 5-7

[4]   Numbers 5:1-4

[5]   2 Samuel 11:2-5

[6]   Luke 22:3-6

[7]   Hebrews 11:17

God kills en masse,[8],[9],[10],[11] choosing to apply the principle of mercy almost exclusively to those who happen to be "blessed" under the umbrella of God's covenant by association.[12] Surely, serendipitous association with a higher power's contract is not the best way to judge that a tribe is deserving of mercy. It leaves the unluckily unassociated in a very unfortunate position.

What is the problem? I have already dealt with the argument of figurative interpretation. Still, some argue that we simply do not understand the reasons for those actions. I honestly do not feel that this is too important. Suppose that God told the Israelites to slaughter and pillage the Midianites (and their male infants, conveniently sparing the virgin girls),[13] because failing to do so would trigger an immediate apocalypse into an underworld of chaos, where even the Israelites would be constantly tormented. Obviously, this was not the case. Yet, even if it were, we would still not feel well about the whole murdering, raping, and stealing situation.

We should make a distinction between actions that are *admissible*, and actions that are *justifiable*. The former is about compromise, and the latter is about virtue, purity, and faultlessness. No amount of typology or reasoning exempts a perfectly loving and just God from actions that are clearly more admissible than justifiable.

---

[8]   Exodus 12:29

[9]   Joshua 6:20-21

[10]   1 Samuel 15:2-3,7-8

[11]   Hosea 13:16

[12]   Genesis 7:23

[13]   Numbers 31:1-54

This is the problem: if we are supposed to be taught morality from the Bible, why do we feel conflicted? If there is such thing as a "moral compass," then it does not originate from, or point in the same direction as, the morality suggested by the Bible. What makes this worse is that God does actually provide laws to ensure righteous conduct, such as the Ten Commandments.[14] Yet, they are readily broken through God's own commands, such as in the pillaging that God commanded the Israelites of over the Midianites.[15]

Consider another example. A man single-handedly commits genocide while raping entire groups of women, and goes to prison. Because of one prayer in prison, he is spared all judgement by God because his sin is already judged with Jesus. This situation does not lend itself to any obvious moral insights. However, it should cause some confusion since most of us intrinsically feel uncomfortable about the fact that the man is unambiguously spared all judgement.

Time and time again, our moral intuitions, which are supposedly programmed by God, come into conflict with Biblical morality.

Actions that are otherwise clearly wrong can be done on a well-established biblical basis.

Again, our moral compasses are often incompatible with the Bible's suggestions of morality. For instance, the Bible

---

[14] Exodus 20:1-17
[15] Numbers 31:1-54

does not speak out against slavery, or the combination of powerful appointments with financial authority. I point this out making the assumption that most (if not all) of us feel intrinsically that there is something wrong with them.

If anything, the Bible seems to condone these kinds of practices. In fact, the Bible provides guidelines for the treatment of slaves, both from the Old and New Testaments. [16,17,18,19,20,21] While we might be able to find some verses that seem to criticize certain practices associated with slavery,[22] it is nevertheless true that the Bible still provides guidelines for, and appears to approve of, slavery, in the sense that a man might purchase and trade another as his own property.[23]

Some people claim that the Bible does not clearly approve of slavery, but rather that God provided guidelines for a practice that was already commonplace. However, the absence of criticism against the practice, commonplace or not, combined with its provision of guidelines to those who practiced it, should be enough evidence to suggest that the Bible appears to condone slavery.

The Bible also seems to condone situations where powerful people are given great control over finances, amongst other kinds of power and influence. Religious leaders are also the political and financial rulers. King Solomon, in

---

[16]   Deuteronomy 23:15

[17]   Exodus 21:1-36

[18]   Leviticus 22:11

[19]   Colossians 4:1

[20]   Ephesians 6:5

[21]   Titus 2:9-10

[22]   Exodus 21:16

[23]   Leviticus 25:44-46

particular, was supposedly richer than any other man who lived before him.[24] The rulers of tribes also received offerings "on behalf" of God,[25] in situations where they would be able to conveniently feast off of the best produce from their tribes.

Faith is a dangerous, misunderstood, and misapplied idea, and is mostly useless towards any positive aim.

I am not hyperbolizing here, but I might be misunderstood because my claim is inherently a divisive one. I am not implying that faith is uncompromisingly irreconcilable with reason in any context, but that we should have a grasp of what faith actually is, and know where it falls short of being useful to us so that we can maximize its utility and minimize its harm. Here, I will:

1. Decide on a reasonable and workable definition of faith.
2. Show how the definition can be used to distinguish between claims made on the basis of faith, and claims not made on the basis of faith.
3. Explain why it is dangerous.
4. Show where faith can occasionally be put to good use, and why—even in that case—faith should not be viewed in an endearing light.

---

[24] 1 Kings 3:13
[25] Numbers 7:1-89

There are many religious and secular definitions for the idea of faith. Since its boundaries are very difficult to draw, I'd like to propose a definition that is understandable and workable from any angle.

To illustrate the ambiguity of more complex definitions, one might choose to reference Hebrews 11:1 (KJV), which says, "Now faith is the substance of things hoped for, the evidence of things not seen." It should go without saying that it is very difficult to agree on an understandable interpretation of what is written in this particular verse well enough to form an agreeable definition of what faith is. I propose, much more simply, that **faith is any belief formed in the absence of evidence.** Many dictionaries will give similar definitions, such as this one that I found online: "… [faith is] belief that is not based on proof." To use any of the other definitions provided would cause any discussion to either be too confusing or unnecessary. For example, if one chooses to define faith as any religious belief or "confidence or trust", then there is really no point in using the word faith in the first place.

Having now established a useful definition of faith, we can attempt to understand how this idea fits into the decisions that we make about reasonability, evidence, and beliefs in general.

First, we need to decide on what this definition encompasses. Consider the following context:

We trust that mathematics (or, at the very least, basic algebra and equations) accurately reflects the reality that we exist in. We can easily agree that this is true, regardless of philosophical bias, and that our confidence in mathematics is not a matter of faith, despite the fact that we cannot conclusively disprove the claim that a new, untested mathematical calculation will not reflect this reality.

Suppose that we have a particular equation, 2.01x=4, and that the number, 2.01, happens to have never been multiplied or divided in the history of mathematics. I'd choose a better number if it didn't complicate the example. Furthermore, there will be no actual way to test our estimation of this value against reality.

A critic of mathematics will now posit that, since we have never done this before, we cannot simply assume to solve for x by the calculation, 4/2.01, where our estimation of x reflects the actual value of x in reality.

Our claim, of course, would be that the solved value of x *would indeed reflect its actual value*. Should we say that is a claim of faith? Our definition stipulates that a faith-claim is one that occurs in the absence of evidence. Certainly, there is evidence to back up this claim. Nevertheless, the evidence is still imperfect. We are unable to provide *any* concrete proof that this calculation will absolutely produce the real value of x, since we cannot see the future. All we can do is make the assumption that the laws of nature and mathematics are extremely unlikely to suddenly change, since they have not done so to us yet. Notice that this definite "lack of evidence" does not constitute enough of an absence of evidence for us to apply the label of faith.

The purpose of this illustration is to point out that we make assumptions all the time, and that many of these assumptions must be made with the existence of the absence of perfect and complete evidence. Nevertheless, the absence of perfect and complete evidence is not the same as a *total* absence of evidence. Therefore, we make claims that—for the most part—cannot be considered faith claims.

A true faith claim would be one where there really is no reason or evidence to suggest that it is even likely. For instance, I might suggest eating cow lungs to generate magic powers. *That* would clearly be a faith claim.

This distinction is the basis of my next point, which is that many religious beliefs, which are considered to be ones of faith, are actually claims of fact and reason. I will go back to Hebrews 11 to make my point, assuming that all of the stories were actually true, so that my phrasing will not be burdened by the constant need to qualify my statements.

Hebrews 11:17 (NKJV) says, "By faith Abraham, when he was tested, offered up Isaac..." This is the famous story of Abraham willingly sacrificing his own son out of obedience to the command of God. Typology aside, Christians are all too familiar with various reasons that Abraham might have had to sacrifice his son. After all, that would quite clearly be an abysmally gruesome idea.

For example, God told Abraham that his descendants would be as numerous as the stars in the sky.[26] Abraham would have been sure that those descendants would come through Isaac because he was the child that God promised; in fact, even his conception was miraculous.[27] As a result, Abraham would have been confident that God would not let Isaac be killed, or, alternatively, that he would have been resurrected even if he was killed.

---

[26]   Genesis 26:4

[27]   Genesis 17:20-21

This is certainly not a claim of faith. Abraham would have been convinced that the act of giving up Isaac was a good idea purely by the basis of reason. This was reason, and not faith.

Hebrews 11:11 (NKJV) is an even clearer case: "By faith Sarah herself also received strength to conceive seed, and she bore a child when she was past the age, because she judged Him faithful who had promised." If Sarah judged God, who promised her a child, to be faithful, then that is a reason, and therefore not faith.

Of course, this does not mean that the verse is intrinsically contradictory, given that the writer is free to define "faith" as he pleases. However, this definition of faith is not useful to us, as I have illustrated with the example about mathematics. Here, we might better understand the use of the word "faith" by replacing it with the words "confident belief," which clearly has nothing to do with whether or not the belief is based on concrete evidence.

These are but two examples of reason disguised as faith. Here, it may be tempting to argue that the Bible's use of the word "faith" *actually means* "confident belief." However, I adhere to my own definition because it is the one that people actually understand to be faith. Any other definitions, such as "confident belief," seem unnecessary because their validity would eliminate the need for such a profoundly spiritual word.

Sermons are preached and doctrines are taught making the assumption that faith does *not* merely refer to a confident belief, but, rather, a confident belief that lacks concrete evidence. Preachers rely on the concept of the absence of observed certainty to portray the idea of faith as something that is awe-inspiring.

Another way to look at this conflict might be to conclude that "faith" does not actually mean what everybody *thinks* it means. As a result, though, we would need to completely re-examine our understanding of the doctrine of faith in Christianity. Of course, regardless of how this issue is finally dealt with, the conflict exposes the fact that there is, surely, something wrong about either our understanding of faith, or the way that the Bible has been written. It might be said that there is either a problem with the practice of the religion, or the religion itself (or both?).

Now I will give examples of belief in the bible that we *can* interpret within the definition that I have provided. They are frequently used in sermons concerning faith.

Here are the words of Jesus in the book of John 20:29 (NKJV): "Jesus said to him, 'Thomas, because you have seen Me, you have believed. Blessed are those who have not seen and yet have believed.'" This verse is often quoted to describe faith, and it fits the definition that I have provided. There are many popular interpretations of this passage, but I feel that faith, in the way that I've defined it, is the best.

These are also Jesus' words, but this time in Luke 17:6 (NKJV): "So the Lord said, 'If you have faith as a mustard seed, you can say to this mulberry tree, 'Be pulled up by the roots and be planted in the sea,' and it would obey you...'" This is, again, faith, in the sense that one believes without good evidence to show that it should happen.

Having covered the issue of ambiguity, I will proceed to explain why I say that faith is a dangerous idea. We are often presented with the assertion that faith is a virtue. In fact, that is unequivocally what the Christian Bible says. The first one that comes to mind is Hebrews 10:38 (KJV),

"Now the just shall live by faith..." However, we should be wary of any suspension of reason, because it is the necessary mechanism that gives way to dogma.

Dogma may manifest itself in a number of ways, but there is no way to stop it from manifesting in a dangerous way, such as Nazism, or the North Korean worship of the Kims. The primary mechanism that gives way to—and perpetuates—such circumstances is faith. Although dogma may sometimes manifest itself in a relatively benign manner, it is still extremely dangerous because we cannot ensure that it will not manifest with a harmful result. Whatever faith happens to actually be, it is surely not a virtue.

Of course, that does not mean that we must necessarily dispense of faith in all situations. In fact, it may be useful to "hope against hope," if I may borrow that biblical expression, in a future where everybody is happier and better off. There is no good reason to ever suspect that everybody will necessarily be better off. Nevertheless, allowing ourselves to temporarily believe and imagine it can prove useful to lift our spirits. Of course, the caveat here is that I am promoting a *controlled* delusion, which is to say that delusion might actually be useful, so long as it is intentional, temporary, and contained.

I hope that I have been able to authentically represent the concept of faith to whatever extent possible on paper, and demystify any unnecessarily euphemized or venerated connotations that might be forced into religious association with faith.

QUESTIONABLE REASONING

As a Christian, I noticed (with incredible discomfort) that almost everyone prioritized preferred conclusions over better reasoning. This kind of belief system seemed to invariably give rise to pseudo-scientific claims at every church; it was just a matter of time.

My favorite example is laminins. Laminins are a set of proteins which are a necessary part of almost all of our cells and organs. The distinguishing feature of laminins, with respect to Christianity, is that they are shaped like a cross. Large groups of Christians have taken our understanding of laminins to mean that Christ *literally* holds human beings together.

Of course, if we were to say that laminins were evidence *for* God, we would also be saying that the absence of laminins would be evidence *against* God, which is clearly not the case (or so I think). We see in this situation an unfair willingness to accept bad reasons for a preferred conclusion.

In this chapter, I will deal with observations of questionable reasoning that I have made, based on what I experienced in Christian churches.

Christian claims are either not properly testable, or are otherwise relatively meaningless.

This is a particularly difficult idea to express. My best attempt will have to be to give a few examples. The first is something that seems to have originated at one of the churches that I had attended, but the second and third will be more common amongst churches.

The reason that these kinds of claims are disheartening is that they are characteristic of delusions: self-verifying false beliefs.

"Right believing gives birth to right living."

Clearly, this is claimed in a religious or spiritual context. That is to say that a proper, Biblical claim will result in better behavior than would have otherwise resulted, all other factors remaining equal. That is, at least, what I understand to be implied.

I take issue with the fact that many Christians are not willing to allow a clear, tangible definition of such a statement. Although we should avoid paraphrasing when unnecessary, it seems very obvious that it *is* necessary here. What does somebody mean when they say that "right believing gives birth to right living?" Unless there are tangible causes and effects, the claim merely reduces to nice words that I cannot understand.

I will restate my paraphrasing of this statement: a proper, Biblical claim will result in better behavior than would have otherwise resulted, all other factors remaining equal.

The statement that I've made should put the problem into perspective. Now that we have a claim, we can test its parts against reality. Of course, I suspect that it will not hold—especially the "Biblical" part.

"His presence is here."

What does it mean that "His presence is here?" Sometimes, I even hear preachers saying: "Do you feel His presence?" If there is something that can be felt, then clearly there is a tangible, physical change in reality. As a result, if this is true, we should be able to measure a change in reality that is contingent upon "God's presence" being present. Again, I doubt that we'd be able to measure any physical changes within a gathering area when such a claim is made.

"God Heals."

Healing is one of the more controversial claims that is difficult to properly test. Regardless of denomination, I find that most Christians are willing to believe that "God heals," whatever that means. What bothers me is that this claim is conveniently untestable, since we cannot ever define the conditions under which God heals. It is merely taken as a matter of faith. Yet, when a religious person happens to witness an unexpected recovery from illness, it is automatically labelled as God's healing. The irony is that when a religious person happens to witness an unexpected fatality from minor illness, it is understood as "part of God's divine plan." Not only is the definition ambiguous, but all results of any potential tests verify the hypothesis. By definition, that is self-verifying.

Self-delusion is very possible.

One of the reasons that people are religious is that seemingly supernatural experiences arise. A Christian might receive a "word of wisdom" while praying for another member in church. The beneficiary will likely recall that, for example, God told him to choose church counselling rather than secular counselling for his relationship problems, and all through a friend who could not have possibly known that he was in such a situation.

Here, a common mistake is made. We assume that any and all illusions present in such situations are the result of conscious manipulation. In this case, that would be the man who prayed and received the word of wisdom. If this were the case, then it might be reasonable to conclude that something incredible really happened.

However, the truth is that illusions can be created easily, repeatedly, and unintentionally. It is not at all unlikely that both participants were completely unaware of any illusions that they created or perpetuated. Situations like this happen all the time, and across religious boundaries.

I will describe one likely way that this situation could have actually played out. The first man would have laid his hands on his friend's shoulders, and prayed for God to freely speak through him. The image of a church would have arisen into consciousness, and he would have said, "God is telling me, 'Church.'" The friend would have then interpreted that as God telling him to choose Christian counselling rather than secular counselling.

Consider that this example did not require any external manipulation. The man praying did not have to be primed to think about a church. He could have imagined any Christian symbol, or something that happened to sound relevant, such as a secular public school, a Christian (or non-Christian) friend, or even a fruit—that last one would be particularly interesting if their preacher would have happened to teach about spiritual "fruits" during their services. Also, the example did not prerequisite the friend's consciousness being overwhelmed by the thought of his struggling relationship. It would have only required that whatever word or image mentioned trigger that thought.

Magicians and con-artists exploit the fact that we add meaning to vaguely-relevant suggestions, and that we often remember those suggestions being much more detailed than they actually were. However, this kind of self-delusion is often caused unintentionally across various types of experiences such as prayer, "extra-sensory perception," and UFO sightings. Self-delusion is not only possible, but it is also a very common religious experience.

Testimony is not good evidence.

Every church that I've attended produces testimonies for the edification of its members and guests. This seems like a perfectly reasonable thing to do. However, it is problematic whenever testimonies are taken to be evidence of supernatural events. It is a fallacy to assume that two events are causally linked simply because they happen in succession, except when there is evidence to show it.

A prayer followed by unusual healing may be as causally linked as eating a Double Quarter Pounder before bumping into a good friend, even if it has happened more than once.

This is still true even when leaders point out that testimonies do not constitute evidence because they warp the member's perceptions of reality. It may not necessarily be the case that tithing more results in better career opportunities. Yet, well-intentioned testimony videos that repeatedly show this kind of situation are clearly dangerous. The result is that, regardless of intention, testimonies warp the members' perceptions of reality, and may directly cause their behavior to change for the worse.

This technique is shared by marketers, charlatans, and propaganda artists. It does not matter that the actor is benevolent; testimony, taken as evidence, is extremely dangerous. Even when the use of testimony is justified, it is necessary to acknowledge that it is a loaded weapon, and that it should be treated with much caution. Testimony can be useful, but it is certainly not good evidence.

Religion is not subject to rigorous self-criticism.

Because of the nature of its activities, religion is not subject to rigorous self-criticism. Sermons and teaching materials introduce ideas as facts, and do not need to show any evidence. On top of that, congregations will not end up looking into the acceptability of these claims, for various reasons. Even when churches attempt to nurture a culture of careful skepticism, the fact of the matter is that claims are not sufficiently challenged or verified.

The result is that a whole lot of odd claims become commonplace beliefs, like the unverified stories of conveniently impressive healing preachers. There are those such as John G. Lake, whose tales—which I still hear of in sermons—are as of yet uninvestigated (so far as I know), and Peter Popoff, who was popular and well-respected until secular investigators showed that he was a fraud, despite the remarkable stories of people who had already claimed their "healing."

I used to think that if the mainstream Christian gospel were true, God would intervene when necessary to ensure that this sort of thing wouldn't happen. Clearly, that's not the case.

Doctrines nurture an unwillingness to accept scientific truth.

The Church has been characteristically slow to accept scientifically-tested truths. The history behind this is very well-known, but I will use this space to briefly recap some of the major points of conflict that had arisen.

Galileo was tried for heresy by the Roman Inquisition for claiming that the Earth revolves around the sun, and not the other way around. It took the Roman Catholic

Church, with the arrival of Pope John Paul II[28], nearly four centuries to admit that this was wrong. It is kind of interesting that, as of 1999, a Gallup poll[29] showed that 18% of their American participants believed that the sun revolves around the Earth. I am not aware of any more recent polls on the same question, but that is disturbing nonetheless.

Charles Darwin published *On the Origin of Species* in 1859.[30] To this day, large groups of Christians, led by their pastors, denounce evolution, despite that fact that there is an abundance of reliable evidence. All signs point to evolution; for instance, not a single fossil has ever been found out of its appropriate strata.[31]

Many Christian groups claim that the flood (as in the "Noah's ark" story in the book of Genesis) literally happened, and that the world is less than 10,000 years old. These groups usually estimate the age of the Earth to be around 5,000 to 6,000 years, based on the genealogies provided in the Bible. These claims are, in particular, impossible to verify through any scientific measurements. By any measurements that we have, the world is 4.5 billion years old;[32] even when we measure the age of rocks and valleys, geologists speak in terms of millions and billions of years. All of our observations show us that the Earth is

---

[28] http://www.livescience.com/27790-catholic-church-and-science-history.html

[29] http://www.gallup.com/poll/3742/new-poll-gauges-americans-general-knowledge-levels.aspx

[30] http://en.wikipedia.org/wiki/On_the_Origin_of_Species

[31] Coyne, Jerry A. (2009). *Why Evolution is True*. Viking. pp. 26–28. ISBN 978-0-670-02053-9.

[32] http://en.wikipedia.org/wiki/Earth

certainly *not* less than four billion years old. Even if all of our measurements were rounded off to the wrong figures, the world still wouldn't be any less than a few billion years old.

If the Church is, indeed, the purveyor of truth, then it should surprise us that it has so often been diametrically opposed to scientific truths. Even to this day, Christian teachings nurture an unnecessarily distrustful attitude towards scientific findings.

Moderate interpretations do not work.

I have only briefly mentioned that I was a Biblical inerrantist, which means that I held that all parts of the Bible were literally true, unless it was otherwise specified to be so by the text itself. Many people have no qualms with calling this sort of belief "fundamentalism," as inerrantism does, in fact, seem to be characterized as such under some formal definitions. Whatever the case may be, the fact is that there is a sizable group of Christians who take it to be true that everything that the Bible says is to be literally understood. As such, the universe would have been necessarily created in six days (24 hours or not).

Of course, it would still allow for obvious exceptions such as John's book of Revelation. This is because it is clearly not meant to be taken literally. For one, John repeatedly says, "I saw," in a fashion that still allows us to interpret his vision as *purely* a vision, as opposed to saying, "there will be," or something similar. Additionally, Jesus explains to John that the stars and lampstands in the vision represent the angels of the seven churches and the seven churches themselves, respectively.

What this means is that the book of Revelation is, at its simplest level, John's account of the vision that he had, and not necessarily a literal prophesy of the last days. However, it should be noted that this is only possible because the text specifically describes itself as the account of a vision, rather than as prophesy. In the absence of such qualifying statements, we would be forced to read it as if it were prophesy.

Most non-Christians will immediately feel that there is something clearly wrong with a literal interpretation of the Bible. On top of that, there are plenty of genuine Christians who will also gladly take opposition to Biblical inerrantism. Yet, for Christians who are in the position that I once was, it may be difficult to see why. If that is the case with you, then it might be useful to follow a thought experiment with me. All that it involves is that we honestly give an account of what happened in the Bible, reporting as if to those who have never heard of it. For the purposes of this illustration, I will limit my scope to the creation story, the fall of man, and the gospel story. How much would your description vary from my own?

"Tell me about the Bible's account of creation."

The Bible begins with the book of Genesis. In the beginning, there was God, but no universe. So, God spoke the universe and the Earth into existence in six days, and rested on the seventh. On each of the six days, He, by speaking, created different things. However, on the sixth day, God specially shaped Adam, in God's own image, from the dust, placed Adam in the Garden of Eden, and then breathed life into Adam. To show that he was to have dominion over creation, he named each and every animal. Following that, God created Eve out of Adam's rib to be Adam's companion.

"What is Original Sin?"

God put a tree, the Tree of Knowledge, by the Tree of Life, in the midst of the Garden of Eden so that Adam and Eve would have a mechanism to demonstrate their obedience to God. Without it, Adam and Eve would only have been able to choose God. The deal was that they were allowed to take from every single tree in the expansive Garden of Eden except for the Tree of Knowledge. Unfortunately, Adam and Eve, through some manipulation by the cunning Serpent, broke that contract. As a result, they were all expelled and barred from returning to the Garden. One of the consequences that followed from the breaching of this contract was that this single sin would taint the blood of every human offspring, forever. As a result, all men have been, and are, born sinful, and are destined to be sentenced to an eternity of damnation, better known as hell. No human effort or "merit" is sufficient to allow him to earn his way back into heaven.

"That sounds pretty grim... Did God provide a solution?"

Yes. Thankfully, God provided a way out for His faithful followers. Initially, the primary method of cleansing the sin of the Israelites (God's people) was through both individual and collective lamb sacrifices, where the blood of an unblemished lamb was to be shed so that the offerer's sin would be exchanged for the unblemished lamb's purity. Additionally, God also judged the Israelites by the holiness of the head priest, so that the priest could carry a heavier burden of obedience on behalf of the people. However, this method of sin-cleansing was temporary, in the way that credit cards are used temporarily. In the end, somebody would still have to foot the bill.

"So, what was the solution? Clearly, we don't sacrifice lamb like that anymore."

In order to end this cycle of temporary cleansing forever, God (the Father) sent Jesus, who is both God and the only Son of God the Father. God sent an angel to the virgin, Mary, to tell her that she would become pregnant with God incarnate, and so it was. Mary gave birth, assisted by her husband, Joseph, in a barn in Bethlehem. Some astrologers (frequently described as being three wise men or kings) happened to find their way to the barn to greet the baby Jesus with gifts of gold, frankincense, and myrrh. Mary and Joseph managed to help Jesus escape the mass infanticide ordered by King Herod, and grew up to be very wise. Jesus began his ministry in his early thirties, amassing a huge following and demonstrating his divinity through miracles such as turning water into wine, healing all sorts of diseases, and feeding thousands with a handful of fish and bread.

Eventually, Judas, one of Jesus' twelve disciples, betrayed him for a bribe paid by the chief priests. After some quarreling between the Jewish people and Pontius Pilate, Pilate agreed to have Jesus scourged. Following the gruesome scouring, the Jewish people also convinced Pilate to, unwillingly, crucify Jesus, as per Roman customs. Jesus was forced to wear a crown of thorns, carry the cross to Golgotha (although he eventually received one person's help on the way), and die a sinner's death on the cross. When he died, there was darkness, an Earthquake, and a resurrection of many saints, who appeared in the city.[33] Three days later, he rose from the dead (commonly celebrated on Easter Sunday), appeared to his disciples, and rose to heaven in his resurrected body (commonly referred to as the "ascension").

Man is born sinful, and cannot merit his way to heaven. However, Jesus took the place of all sinners, and died a death for all sin (past, present, and future), in the way that the sacrificial lamb would have died for a temporary cleansing of sin, so that we can receive his righteousness for our sinfulness. Since the price has already been fully paid at the cross, we can receive perfect righteousness by simply accepting the gift of Jesus' sacrifice on the cross. Typically, we pray a "sinner's prayer" to receive

---

[33] Matthew 27:51-53

this perfect, eternal righteousness, which cannot be sinned away, but I will not put that here, since evangelism is not my intention.

The average Christian should feel slightly odd, perhaps even a bit uncomfortable, when describing certain details of this story. My guess is that it is because we know how rational people will react. Think about how there is a talking *snake*, animal sacrifice, a *virgin* birth, mass infanticide, unimaginable miracles, scourging and crucifying on behalf of mankind, and, last but not least, *multiple* resurrections.

There is an impossible, incredible detail at every turn. Only a delusional person would take these kinds of details as evidence for an even more incredible claim of divine inspiration. Consider how, when conspiracy theorists are presented with contradictory evidence, they take it as evidence *for* their theories, especially because it can be explained that the conspiring authorities are responding to them by producing "fake" evidence.

These miraculous claims would be immediately dismissed as ludicrous if they were made in a modern context. Yet, for whatever reason, placing these assertions in a pre-Christian era increases, in a way that I feel is irrational, their believability.

On top of that, there are certain details that are clearly false. There is no possible way that the Earth is less than 10,000 years old, for instance, unless we were to assume that God had intentionally made creation to seem *as if* it were billions of years old. It is also clearly false that there were any major earthquakes or mass resurrections at the time described by Matthew, in his gospel.

No reliable accounts of history from that period even *mention* any form of earthquakes or mass resurrections, despite how significant those events would have been. Their accounts simply describe routine occurrences, without any sudden interruptions.

If this is the case, then it seems that the reasonable conclusion is to rule out a *purely* literal interpretation of the Bible. That is to say that we are still free, if we see it fit, to interpret *some* parts of the Bible literally, but that not *all* parts can be interpreted literally.

Yet, the dichotomy is that I cannot understand how we should interpret the Bible in any non-literal fashion. This is because there are certain passages that *must* be taken literally, if Christian doctrine is to mean anything at all. The issue is that many of these passages are difficult to reconcile as being literally true, which leads me to the conclusion that there is *no* good way to interpret the Bible while still believing it to be true.

For example, the Genesis account of creation *must* be interpreted as literal if Original Sin is to have any effect at all. This doctrine relies on Adam and Eve literally sinning in the Garden of Eden. If we interpret the creation story as a metaphor for the natural development of creation, then the story of Adam and Eve must also be taken metaphorically, since man would have purposelessly evolved into existence.

Many people have found ways to try and reconcile this conflict. For instance, a Methodist pastor that I spoke to explained to me that there were probably two critical moments of creation, where God would intervene.

The first would be a first cause, in the sense that God would be involved only for a moment, and then spark the natural progression of creation. Following that, God would have intervened once more in a special moment of creation to form Adam and Eve at the opportune moment.

Of course, my qualm with this kind of interpretation is that it is obviously insincere, contrived, and unnecessarily complex. Never mind the fact that this is the kind of reasoning that conspiracy theorists argue from, this interpretation raises as many questions as it purports to answer.

If nature was allowed to develop on its own, then where did the Garden of Eden come from? On top of that, why did God punish Eve by creating birth pains if birth pains would have already existed? How come there was a talking snake if snakes were not part of this special moment of divine intervention?

What I have established is that the Bible, at some parts, must be interpreted literally in order for Christian doctrines to have meaning. Yet, it is clear that many of those passages should not be interpreted as such. Therefore, we are left, by means of elimination, only with the possibility that the Bible is *not* the revealed Word of God, as according to Christians. The Bible may often be good literature, but it is *not* divine.

OBSERVATIONS OF
INCOHERENCE

As a Christian, I was confused by my observations on a number of fronts. The ideas that I will be covering in this chapter were amongst the most confusing. Many of these observations made no sense at all, except when I lifted away the assumption that the Bible was the revealed Word of God.

Trickery and manipulation within Christianity is rather difficult to distinguish from the "legitimate" faith.

I've mentioned already that self-delusion is very possible. There, I explained one example of self-delusion, resulting from the human tendency to add meaning to suggestions, where additional meaning is non-existent. This is also the case in other situations such as faith healing. Although I could probably give examples of trickery and manipulation through faith healing, I would recommend watching some videos of these tricks in action, which is much more interesting. My favorite is a documentary by Derren Brown called *Miracles for Sale*.

It is quite clear that these kinds of con-artists do not define the religion, and that Christianity is not characterized by manipulation. However, it should also be acknowledged that trickery and manipulation is very difficult to distinguish from the actual faith. That does not necessarily mean that the practice of Christianity is full of illusion. However, the fact that these things happen should cause Christians to become more skeptical of their beliefs, especially if their churches happen to practice activities that seem similar.

Christianity is often irrelevant.

Christian teachings, like those of many other religions, are often irrelevant. Spending time amongst groups of people who happen to not be Christian makes this more obvious. At no point have I ever found that it was ever absolutely necessary to refer to ideas or beliefs that were specifically Christian (or Muslim, or Jew, or Buddhist, or Sikh) in order to make any kind of progress. Entire societies function well without needing to draw from the doctrines of any religion, of which Christianity belongs. The world's governments rely on secular reasoning to produce their best policies, and our greatest medical advances are based on secular science.

If Christianity is as real as its believers claim it to be, we should then expect its teachings and doctrines to at least be more relevant than those of other religions, if not secular reason. For instance, Christianity would be more relevant if we could observe that Christian prayers were consistently more effective at healing cancer than other religious or secular methods. Of course, this is an absurd claim, but my argument is that relevance is, necessarily, both *observable* and *repeatable*.

Ironically, it was a Christian testimony that really helped hit this idea home for me. During a regular cell-group session, I listened to my friend share about her week. It was a stressful week—even by junior college standards—because she had just sat through multiple assessments. Her testimony was that, through God's help, she encouraged herself so much so that she was able to encourage her friends.

What struck me as interesting, though, was the method by which her friends' spirits were uplifted. She said that she shared God's divine messages in secular form to her friends. If God told her to relax because the results had already been prophesied, she would tell her friends to relax because stressing out would not do anything to improve their results. I was taken by surprise when I realized that these words of encouragement seemed to be as effective as each other. If that was the case, then divinity did not actually make much of a difference—or, at least, I could not detect any significant differences.

The fact of the matter is that when a sect of society proves that its own idea is reliable and truthful, that idea ceases to belong to itself, and becomes part of a larger body of collective human knowledge. This is, and has been, the case with medicine: if an alternative medicine is proven reliable through rigorous testing, it ceases to be alternative. When Muslim intellectuals created modern algebra, and it proved useful, it ceased to fall under the umbrella of Islam (if it ever did at all), and became an established mathematical practice.[34] This was also the case with the Hindu-Arabic numeral system (0, 1, 2, 3...), which is now a primary mathematical tool used by the masses.[35]

Our body of shared human knowledge, across sectarian boundaries, is characterized by a distinct absence of supernatural claims, including those of Christianity, because these claims do not serve to effectively answer any important questions about the reality in which we exist. In stark contrast, irrespective of the individuals' religions or philosophical affiliations, modern civilizations function most effectively on the foundation of proper mathematics, science, and secular reason.

Even if we agreed to hold the assumption that Christianity were relevant, we would be distraught by another problem, because we would not know *which* Christianity were, indeed, relevant. There are many different versions of doctrines and beliefs within Christianity, even amongst those beliefs that should be core to the faith. For instance, denominations still disagree significantly about the extent to which salvation— in the narrow sense that it refers to escaping damnation and entering heaven—is permanently attained. This means

---

[34] Rosen, Fredrick (1831). The Algebra of Mohammed Ben Musa. Kessinger Publishing. ISBN 1-1179-4914-7.

[35] Collier's encyclopedia, with bibliography and index William Darrach Halsey, Emanuel Friedman - 1983.

that we are unable to *absolutely* ascertain which teachings belong to the *actual* Christianity, should there actually be an original one in the first place.

The pervasive irrelevance of Christianity, coupled with its characteristically unclear teachings, should cause us to become more skeptical about its actuality.

Free will is not a coherent idea.

Our intuitions lead us to believe that we have free will. However, this assumption breaks down in the light of a closer examination. I will explain what I used to think about free will, what free will actually is like, and why this observation is incongruent with mainstream Christian doctrine.

Seemingly by default, I had always simplistically expected that all human beings were able to choose freely between all available choices, which would also imply that all choices were as freely open to choice as each other. For instance, if I were given a choice between red and blue, I could then choose red just as easily as I could decide on blue. Another context might be that heads would be just as available to choose to me as tails. In these simple examples, that expectation certainly holds true, which is probably a good reason why it had really never crossed my mind that this was a problem at all.

Nevertheless, upon some further consideration, that expectation breaks down in the face of reality because it holds two false assumptions.

1: Availability of Choices

The more obvious of these two assumptions is that all choices are available to us. Of course, the obvious truth is that I cannot choose what I am not aware of. If I am unaware that there are other countries to travel to, then I am by default confined to live within my own.

2: Autonomy of self

Secondly, we assume that we have autonomy apart from the deterministic systems that would otherwise control our decisions. In other words, there should be a "me" (spirit, soul, etc.) that is controlling my brain from the outside. I suggest reading Sam Harris's book, *Free Will*, to get a perspective on the different understandings of free will. It is barely fifty pages, and is extremely well-written. There is also an argument about punishment that I think is relevant to this subject, but I won't explain it here.

Basically, all of the dominant academic understandings of free will show us that there is no such thing, in the sense that free will means that there is some part of me that is making an absolutely autonomous decision. This is for two reasons: either our present consciousness is necessarily dependent on a chain of causes that precedes it, and it is not "our" choice, or our present conscious randomly arises, and it is not "our" choice.

In other words, there does not appear to be "free will," in the way that we traditionally understand it. There is merely an illusion of free will, and the main debate is over what we should understand this illusion to be; some feel that the illusion of free will is sufficient to be interpreted as *actual* free will, while others, including Sam Harris, simply take it to mean that there is no such thing apart from the illusion.

Incompatibilities

Now, I will explain two reasons why the truth about free will is incompatible with examples of Christian doctrines.

Firstly, those who have never heard of Jesus Christ, or have never been presented with the choice of "receiving Him as their Lord and Savior," simply do not have the chance of going to heaven, so long as the entrance to heaven is contingent upon the individuals personally accepting Jesus' forgiveness. This includes the developed societies during the early Christian era where the gospel of Jesus Christ had not yet traveled, such as China.

Secondly, based on the way that I understand it, the question of pain and suffering in this world can easily be explained away by attributing its existence to original sin. This method of accounting for pain and suffering seemed to be a very clean and thorough mechanism, which is also probably the reason why I have had so much trouble trying to put this particular idea about free will into words. The idea behind original sin is that God gave Adam and Eve free will, so that they would have the ability to demonstrate their preference for a world under God, as opposed to disobedience towards God.

However, if what we now understand is true, then Adam and Eve could not have had any actual autonomy. As a result, it could be said that God knowingly put Adam and Eve in a situation that would necessarily result in the Fall of Man, and, therefore, pain and suffering in the world.

The unknown is unnecessarily feared.

It is normal to fear the unknown. However, religions (including Christianity) have consistently taught us to nurture an irrational fear of phenomena that are otherwise innocuous, attributing them to supernatural causes.

I grew up doing magic tricks, and what I learned along the way was that a lot of seemingly supernatural activities (like psychic readings and psychokinetic demonstrations) were really just magic tricks. Here is one of my own, original effects: prepare a good handful of non-magnetic coins, one magnetic coin (that you can identify, but that is not too obvious), one strong magnet, one black marker, one small notepad, some matches, and find a stooge.

In advance of your demonstration, you'll need to be seated at an opaque-surfaced table (preferably with a tablecloth draped over its edges), with the magnet on your lap, and the bunch of coins in your pocket (or wherever they would be less suspicious). Your stooge should be able to clearly identify the magnetic coin.

Let me describe how the rest will appear to your audience. The performer decides to grab a bunch of coins for a demonstration, and places them all on the table. He also brings out matches, a small notepad, and a black marker. He turns around and proceeds to give instructions to the audience members.

All the members of the audience will think of a close person who has passed away, but one member will volunteer, who has vivid memories of his own close person. He writes the name of the person on the notepad, tears it off, and keeps it to himself. Another volunteer is asked to take a few coins from the pile, and mark letters on the back of each of these randomly selected coins, before placing them letter-side down on the table into a second pile. One of these coins should bear the initial(s) of the first volunteer's passed loved one. The rest of the coins are pushed aside or discarded.

The performer turns around. He holds a match, at eye level, above the coins, and lights it. As he does so, the first volunteer is asked to close his eyes, vividly recall details about that person, and then blow out the match. The performer drops the match onto the coins, and one coin dramatically slides out by itself. The initials on the back match the initials of the volunteer's loved one, as shown on the sheet from the notepad.

This is a very powerful, emotional demonstration. This is the method:

1. Clearly, the second volunteer will be the stooge.
2. When the first person volunteers, he will identify himself to you, but not the identity of his loved one.
3. The point of the notepad is to quickly divulge the identity of his loved one to the stooge, and, secondly, to keep him occupied. Make sure to ask this volunteer to *print* the name of his loved one, clearly, *across* the page. When he tears it off, the instruction is to hold the folded sheet tight in his hands (for drama). This gives us an excuse for needing a second volunteer.
4. There is a pacing required for the marking of the coins. The script is like this: "Now, take any coin, and print one or two random capital letters on it. Got it? Place it away from the original pile of coins,

and make sure the side with the letter is facing down on the table. Done? Good. Do it with a few more coins, maybe five or six in total. Oh, make sure that one of them has the initials of [the first volunteer]'s loved one."

5. When you mention that one of the coins should have the initials of the loved one, the stooge picks up the magnetic coin, and pretends to forget the initials of that person. He gets the first volunteer to whisper the initials to him. That coin should not be placed between other coins in the pile, so that it will slide out nicely.

6. The match has two functions: it is both a distraction, and a performance tool used to create drama. When it is lit, the act of increasing your concentration on the match gives you a nice cover to drop one hand below the table. It is even better if you can toss the other matches behind you into a bin (your arm is then even more naturally under the table).

7. The final move is a tough sell, but looks amazing if done properly. All you are doing next is using the magnet under the table to make the coin appear as if it has been slid out of the pile by an invisible force (which, in fact, it is). This requires good timing and showmanship.

This kind of demonstration is *explicitly* a magic trick. That is why people are comfortable with treating it as entertainment. What some people do not understand is that *all* of these kinds of demonstrations are magic tricks, whether intentionally conjured or not. This is particularly so in the case of psychics, and it is blatantly obvious to magicians when psychics perform the same kinds of demonstrations as the magicians do.

When Christians assume the existence of supernatural entities, conjuring tricks and illusions (intentional or not, naturally-occurring or not) are assumed to be the effect of these entities. When one illusion is explained, there is suddenly one less supernatural event. When several illusions are explained, the appearance of supernatural events suddenly recedes.

I assert that it is a bad hypothesis that supernatural entities are responsible for unknown phenomena. I only know of situations where the supernatural hypothesis has been disproved, in favor of natural explanations. Can you think of any counter-examples?

Anthropocentrism

The Bible is overwhelmingly anthropocentric, regardless of how it is interpreted. What I mean by this is that the Bible (or the scripts that is comprises) was clearly written *by* people, *about* people, and *for* people. I imagine that quite a few readers will take issue with this statement, since theology requires us to say that the Bible is actually about Jesus. That may possibly be a valid counter-point, but it is rather irrelevant to the idea that I am trying to communicate. Let's look at the details, and perhaps they will speak for themselves.

If we could only learn about reality through the scriptures, we would almost certainly paint a tellingly man-centered picture of the 6000-year-old universe, with Earth at its center, and with man as the pinnacle of God's perfect creation. Contrast that to what modern biology and astronomy have taught us about the universe.

We are one in a multitude of imperfectly-formed species, though locally dominant, on one of several planets, which all revolve around the sun. The sun and this solar system, are almost indistinguishable from the myriad systems that make up our galaxy, the Milky Way. Our solar system is not even at the center of the Milky Way, but on one of its arms!

The Milky Way is one of *hundreds of billions of* galaxies in the *observable* universe, and, for all we know, there could be a multiverse of universes on top of that. Perhaps there are even multiverses of multiverses above them, but anything past the observable universe is already speculation. The point is that, on the scale of the universe, our existence and activities are *not even* a blip on the radar.

We are so insignificant that I cannot drop a pin on any recent picture of the universe to identify our home without also happening to identify *billions* of other potentially similar celestial bodies.

But what is the point of saying all of this? How does this make a difference to me being a Christian (or being *not* a Christian)?

Let me pose a question: how would the Bible sound if it was not the inerrant word of God? On the flip side, how would it sound if it was?

If the Bible was, indeed, as unerring and God-inspired as preachers lead us to believe, I would expect it to reveal to us a picture of the universe of which man is insignificant. I would expect God to reveal to us knowledge that is truly divine—that science would have to catch up to. References to a possibly elliptically-shaped Earth and the importance of blood for survival do not count.

Imagine if the Bible specified that life was borne of a double-helix structure comprised of four nucleobases, or that mass is equivalent to energy by the proportion of light squared; then, I would say that we have something visibly divine (or, at the very least, greater than us) on our hands.

A quick search on the internet will return results that attempt to defend the other side of this debate by claiming to demonstrate the consistency of the Bible with scientific discoveries. Read those defenses, and ask yourself if they sound convincing to you. I would respond to those arguments here, but others have already done so, and in better style than I think I could accomplish. If you are curious, my favorite article is *The Scriptural Basis for a Geocentric Cosmology* by Glenn Elert.

CONCLUSION

Piecing the Puzzle Together

I feel that I have provided *sufficient* and *actionable* data for those who have been too confused by the debate, and it is very important to me that I have done so.

As a Christian, it did not initially bother me that there were so many questions about Christianity that were unanswered, as such answers were not necessary to validate my certainty about God. Rather, I required a disproportionately great amount of confusion to shake my intuition in order for me to challenge my own beliefs. My observations about Christianity painted a picture of reality that did just that. As a result, I ended up asking myself two questions that changed everything:

1. Why is it that reality is less confusing without a Christian perspective?

2. How much evidence would I need to be sure that I am wrong (or right)?

Having already dealt with Pascal's Wager earlier in this book, the two questions that I asked myself about reality become more central to the discussion because they are primarily concerned with understanding reality through evidence. I encourage Christians to take a moment, and to think carefully about their answers to these two questions; they were the ones that really pushed me over the edge.

After much thinking and waiting, I finally realized for myself that reality made much more sense to me through a non-spiritual, non-religious perspective, and that Christian doctrines made my life unnecessarily confusing. My guess is that many people will come to the same conclusion, and I hope that this will be the case with you.

Confused After?

In this book's introduction, I promised that you would have enough certainty to draw "confident and reliable conclusions" about God and the Bible. The honest truth is that we will never have perfect certainty; yet, we can still be certain enough about our conclusions to act on them. This is true about everything that we do on a daily basis. Driving is *potentially* hazardous, but we drive. Restaurant food is *potentially* poisonous, but we eat out. Not believing in God is *potentially* punishable, but many of us are non-religious.

By this point, many of us will already have confidently casted aside the God hypothesis as either irrelevant or misguided. I would like to direct the following comments towards those who find themselves speechless, when confronted by intuition-destroying arguments made in defense of Christianity.

I understand the feeling. I felt it when I left church, and I still feel it when I hear new arguments made in the defense of God. Let's deal with two specific examples of these kinds of arguments, and then move on to making sense of our confused intuitions.

Love

Sitting directly across from me at the coffee table was a Protestant minister who originated from the Catholic Church. I wasn't sure how to begin this conversation, so I directly asked him why he believed in God, and his response left a very deep impression on me: "I believe in the love of God just like I believe that my wife loves me. I can't quantify or demonstrate with evidence that my wife loves me, but I still know it."

I was wrestling with a lot of ideas at that time, and this one really caught me off guard. I didn't know how to respond. I wanted to say to him, "Well, there is evidence that your wife loves you. *That's* why you know that she loves you." However, I didn't say that because I didn't want to come back with a knee-jerk response, which was exactly what that was.

How would you have responded?

Historical Science

Ken Ham is well known for his involvement with the "Creation Museum" in the United States, and for representing young Earth creationism, which basically argues that the world is less than 10,000 years old. He got the most media attention, though, when Bill Nye debated him.

I remember exposing myself to Ham's arguments when I left church, but I remember feeling too confused by the discussions that he was involved in to continue trying to understand his arguments. Looking back, it has become clear why that was the case.

The argument that really stuck in my mind was a philosophical one, where Ham argued that scientists should make a distinction between *historical* and *observational* science. He claims that historical science, referring to ideas such as evolution, are not well substantiated because they should not be studied in the same way that we study observational sciences, such as physics or chemistry.

Prior to exposing myself to Ham's arguments, I had never heard of such a distinction. I began to think that, perhaps, scientists were hiding something from us, but did not give it much thought again until Ham's debate with Nye.

How would you respond to such a claim?

Dealing with Novel Arguments

In both of the examples that I have provided, I was caught off guard by arguments that I had never heard before. First, let's find out why these arguments do not hold up in the light of an honest analysis.

The argument about love is bad for two reasons. Firstly, it argues that we should believe in ideas on the basis of emotion. Secondly, it is a bad argument because there actually *is* evidence to show that one person loves another.

In fact, we are very good at coming up with evidence to show that some spouses do *not* love one another.

Ham's argument about the distinction between historical and observational science is a bad argument because, simply put, it is fabricated. There is actually no such dichotomy, and all sciences rely on the same principles of skeptical inquiry, which require us to adhere to the highest standards of evidence and proof.

Now that we have dealt with these two arguments for what they are, I will explain how we should deal with these kinds of novel arguments.

Novel arguments can catch us off guard, and can confuse our logic, but novel arguments cannot disprove conclusions that have already been established.

It is useful to make the distinction between deductive and inductive arguments. Deductive arguments *must* be true when its premises are true, while inductive arguments *may* be true when its premises are true.

For example, the following is a deductive argument:

> $2x = 1;$
> *Therefore, x =* ½.
> The next argument is inductive:
> *When I drop things, they usually fall towards the ground;*
> *Therefore, when I drop my cup, it will fall towards the ground.*

Why does it help to make the distinction between deductive and inductive arguments? The answer is that once we have established a conclusion by deductive reasoning, it *must* be true, and can no longer be disproved. If it can be disproved, then the deductive reason is flawed.

If you reread arguments two and three under the "From a Christian perspective" subsection of Chapter 2, you'll see that I provided two clear, deductive arguments. The implication is that, when you agree that the premises are true (salvation is only possible from one religion, and so on), it necessarily follows that the Abrahamic God cannot exist.

Conclusions that have already been established through clear, deductive reasoning are not threatened. Therefore, it is *safe* and *reasonable* to think less about arguments that are confusing, so long as their conclusions do not fall in line with conclusions that have already been drawn out of deductive reasoning.

In other words, we can safely ignore novel arguments, and spend more time on *important* and *pivotal* arguments, such as those that I have given in Chapter 2.

What happens next?

If you started this book as a Christian, and finished as a non-religious person, then it's time to move on with life. There are more important things than philosophical and religious debates. We have significant global problems to solve, and chances are that, if you're reading this book, you have the resources to, at the very least, contribute to the solutions.

The human race has made much progress. We began without settlements, clean food and water, medical treatments, technologies, or bodies of knowledge. In this past generation, we've gone to the moon, eradicated smallpox, and spawned the Internet. And those are just some of the things that we've done.

The greatest legacy that we can leave on this world is to build a better home for our descendants, and if we continue with the momentum that has already been building, I believe that we will find ourselves emerging into a future that is even more beautiful than we can imagine. We *can* paint that picture, and I hope that you will do it with me.